Here's Happiness

Robert Schuller

The C. R. Gibson Company
Norwalk, Connecticut 06856

Grateful appreciation is expressed to Word Books for permission to excerpt material in this volume that originally appeared in THE BE (HAPPY) ATTITUDES, copyright © 1985 by Robert H. Schuller, published by Word Books and for material excerpted from SELF ESTEEM, copyright © 1982 by Robert H. Schuller, published by Word Books.

Published by the C. R. Gibson Company
Norwalk, Connecticut 06856
Copyright © 1987 by Word Books
Printed in the United States of America
ISBN 0-8378-1826-5

For information contact:
Word Books
4800 W. Waco Drive
Waco, Texas 76796

Put Jesus at the Helm!

"In the presence of hope—
faith is born.

In the presence of faith—
love becomes a possibility!

In the presence of love—
miracles happen!"

Our Spiritual Doctor

"Who's happy today? Everybody has so many problems!" she snapped.

I had watched the television reporter approach this woman on the streets of New York City. She was obviously over-rushed, over-tense. The interviewer had simply asked her if she was happy. Now all I could see on my screen was the miserable side shot of an ill-mannered, ill-tempered woman whose negative attitude rang in my ears.

I wanted to speak up: *"Wait a minute, whoever you are! Happiness is not a question of having or not having problems. Everyone has problems, and not everyone is unhappy!"*

Happiness is not dependent on whether or not we have problems, any more than it is dependent on whether or not we have material wealth. There are people who are happy even though they have very little. There are also people who are unhappy, even though they have the wealth of kings.

So, where do we find this elusive attitude of happiness? Where do we find escape from the entrapping problems that

rob us of our joy? Where do we find the healing of our wounded hearts?

This question is all important, for too often, too many of us go to the wrong source for help.

I love the story of the man who went to his doctor. The doctor told him, "I'm sure I have the answer to your problem."

The man answered, "I certainly hope so, doctor. I should have come to you long ago."

The doctor asked, "Where did you go before?"

"I went to the pharmacist."

The doctor snidely remarked, "What kind of foolish advice did he give you?"

"He told me to come see you!"

We do go to the wrong places too often. If you have a medical problem, see your physician. If your problem is an unhappy spirit, then I have a spiritual doctor that I recommend. His name is Jesus Christ.

Seek Him First

What does Christ's persecution, crucifixion, and resurrection mean to us? It means that if we allow Christ to live in us, then it will be possible for us, also, to:

Turn our problems into opportunities.

Tackle our opportunities and succeed!

Dream great dreams and make them come true!

Switch from jealousy and self-pity to really caring about others who are much worse off than you are.

Pick up the broken hopes and start over again!

See great possibilities in those unattractive people!

Become a truly beautiful person—like Jesus!

Many doctors suggest taking up an exercise program as the first step on the road to better health. The same principle applies to our spiritual walk. To be pure in heart, we need to take up something:

a dream...

a project...

God's call to do something great!

Our Spiritual First Aid Kit

Most of us have emergency equipment in our homes and offices—a first-aid kit, a flashlight, perhaps a fire extinguisher, at least a telephone with which to call an emergency unit. We prepare for emergencies before they hit, for we never know when they will come and what they will do to us.

As we need to be prepared with physical equipment, we also need to be prepared spiritually before times of persecution arrive. We do that by spending time daily—or, at the very least, weekly—in positive praying, positive Bible study, and worshiping regularly at a positive-thinking church. We saturate our subconscious minds with positive Bible verses, positive hymns, and examples of people who made it through trials successfully, with their faith intact.

Life's Greatest Cause

There is one consuming cause that I can offer you—the cause of Christ in our world today. God is alive, and Christ is alive, and there are millions who are finding Him. If you have not found Him, you have the greatest experience of your life still coming! I offer to you Jesus Christ as your cause.

Take up a "cause," and it's easy to give up "things."

A young married couple living in a cheap little apartment are happy. Why? Because they have a cause—their new married love.

An artist lives in a musty attic—ill-fed, ill-clothed. But he is happy! Why? Because he has a cause to live for...his art. He does not need many material things.

A research scientist who comes to his classroom in baggy pants, with an unshaven face and no tie, isn't interested in expensive suits. He is lost in a cause—that of research and study.

You can get by without a lot of things if you have something great to live for. Jesus said, "Seek first his kingdom and his righteousness, and all these things shall be added unto you" (Matt. 6:33).

Do you want to have a real experience with God? Take up the cross of Jesus Christ. God is offering to you a cause—Christ's cause. Jesus needs you.

Raise the Sail of Faith

Scrawled in the basement of a German home was a Star of David next to these words:

I believe in the sun even when it is not shining.
I believe in love even when I do not feel it.
I believe in God even when He is silent.

"Be My Friend"

In Christianity, we talk about "making a commitment" to Jesus Christ. When we make that commitment, we raise the sail of faith. We sail and make this voyage in our little vessel across the turbulent ocean of life. But remember this: No sail has ever moved a ship. *The wind moves the ship.* The sail only catches the wind.

I'm asking you now to raise the sail of faith, and you will capture and harness the power of the spirit of God.

Now that you have raised that sail of faith, keep it up there, even when you're in the spiritual doldrums. In God's good time the breeze will come. New positive feelings will replace the drab, old, boring, depressing, negative emotions. Fresh enthusiasm for life will come like a brisk breeze surging through you. You will experience a rebirth of youthful joy, energy, and excitement.

Here's how to make all this happen; pray this simple prayer: "Jesus, I need a friend as I journey through life. Right now I'm asking You to be my best friend."

Such was the faith that Job had: "Though God slay me, yet will I trust him."

This faith is sensational! Fantastic! Awesome!

Faith—A Natural Instinct

If you could collect the smartest intellectuals from around the world, bring them together, and ask them one question, "How many of you believe in God?" several hands would go up. On the other hand, many hands would go up if you asked, "How many of you do not believe in God?"

If you divide the smartest, most educated minds of the world into believers and unbelievers, there would be quite a few in each group. That is because faith in God is not a matter of intelligence. Faith is not a result of intellect, any more than it is a result of ignorance.

Faith is not a matter of intelligence. It is a matter of instinct. So if you are struggling with the idea of faith, wise up! Realize that God has planted faith within the instinct of every healthy human being. Just as a healthy bird instinctively takes to the trees, just as a healthy fish swims in the water, so the healthy human being is inclined to be religious. However, just as animals lose some of their innate drives when taken from their natural habitats, so man loses his innate ability to believe in a loving God when he is away too long from positive, faith-producing environments. That is why it is so important to carefully surround ourselves with positive, believing, healthy people.

Religion is a sign of health. Skepticism is a mark of illness. Unbelief is abnormal; belief is normal.

Dr. Gerald Jampolsky, a noted psychiatrist and a dear friend of mine, was for twenty-five years a very strong

agnostic. Then one day, without warning, his life totally changed, and he became a believer in God. I asked him once when we were together, "Dr. Jampolsky, in the years before you were converted, what did you think about people who went to church?"

He said, "For twenty-five years I thought people who went to church, prayed, and believed in God were not normal. I thought they were really kind of sick. Now I see that I was completely wrong. *They* were normal; I was not."

Amid the Darkness—A Shining Faith

Many of you know who Corrie ten Boom was. Either you read the book or you saw the movie of her life, *The Hiding Place.*

Corrie ten Boom participated in an underground railroad in the Netherlands during World War II. Untold numbers of Jews, who were hounded and hunted by the Gestapo, found escape in her house, where they were hidden in a remote, specially constructed room. Corrie, her sister Betsy, and her father hid numbers of Jews who are alive today, but would have been killed in concentration camps. But eventually the Gestapo caught up with the ten Booms. They were sentenced to prison and hence to months of persecution. Here is some of Corrie's testimony.

"I can tell you that I never had experienced such a realization of Jesus being with me as during the time when I was in the concentration camp. Ravensbruck, located north of Berlin in what is now East Germany, is far away from my home in Holland. The barrack where we lived, my sister Betsy and I, was in the shadow of a crematorium. Every day about six hundred bodies were burned there. When I saw smoke go up, I asked myself, 'When will it be my time to be killed?' I did not know beforehand that I should be set free by a miracle of God, and a blunder of man, one week before they killed all the women of my age.

"Sometimes in that terrible concentration camp we had to stand naked; they stripped us of all our clothes. Seven times I went through that ordeal. The first time was the

worst; I could hardly bear it. I never felt so miserable, so cold, so humble. I said to Betsy, 'I cannot bear this.' Then suddenly, it was as if I saw Jesus at the cross. The Bible tells us they took His garments. He hung there naked. By my own suffering I could understand a fraction of the suffering of Jesus, and I was so thankful I could feel as He had felt.

"Jesus was with us, with Betsy and me, at the camp. In the morning we had to stand roll call very early. The chief of our barracks was so cruel that she sent us out a whole hour early. Betsy and I did not go to the square where we would have to stand for hours during roll call; we walked around the tent. Everything was black. The ground was made black with coal. The barracks were painted black. The only light we had was from the stars and the moon. But Jesus was with us; He talked with us and He walked with us. Betsy said something, then He said something. How? I don't know, but we both understood what Jesus said. There was a little bit of heaven in the midst of hell."

God Within Us

Take a look at a fountain pen. The ink flows through it to form words—communication. If you simply give your life to Him today, He can flow through you. He can make your heart right. He can clear the rubbish from your life and replace it with a holy dream! And you'll come to realize that the burning desire, the consuming dream, the strong sense of destiny—yes, all of this inner drive—is the very life of God surging in your soul! Your dream is God within you!

It is a decision! To become a believer! And decide that a positive mental attitude requires that you let the faith flow free.

Some of us complain when God is silent, and doubt His existence. However, we don't stop believing in computers when one is silent because there's a line problem. Don't stop believing in God because you're not hearing from Him at the moment.

Jesus Believed

I believe in God because I choose, like most educated people I know, to listen to the advice of those wiser than myself. And Christ is still unsurpassed even among those persons whose influence in matters of religion stands out supremely in human history. And Christ believed in God. Christ prayed to him, called him Father, and claimed to be in a unique, personal, first-hand knowledge of God's reality. And any doubts I might have about the reality of God quickly lose their power when placed alongside the faith of Christ. To trust my doubts more than the faith of Jesus might well be the height of non-humility—the ultimate display of intellectual arrogance.

Be a Possibility Thinker!

You become a possibility thinker and you begin to say, "I can do all things because I am somebody. I am a friend of Jesus Christ."

The Possibility Thinker's Creed

When faced with a mountain,
I will not quit!
I will keep on striving
until I climb over,
find a pass through,
tunnel underneath,
or simply stay and turn
the mountain into a gold mine—
with God's help!

It takes guts…
…to leave the ruts!

Jesus Was A Possibility Thinker!

To Jesus every problem was a possibility in disguise.

Sickness was an opportunity for healing.

Sin was an opportunity for forgiveness.

Sorrow was an opportunity for compassion.

Personal abuse was an opportunity to leave a good impression and show the world how possibility thinkers react!

To Jesus every person was a gold mine of undiscovered, hidden possibilities!

Peter? A tough-talking fisherman. But—he could make a great leader of a great new church.

Mary Magdalene? A common prostitute. But—she could become a sensitive sweet soul. She could one day anoint His body for burial.

Matthew? A vulgar materialist. But—he had possibilities to become a great writer! Even write a gospel!

To Jesus the important fact about you and me is not that we are sinners, but that we can be saints. So Jesus proclaimed the greatest possibility: The immeasurable MERCY of GOD.

To Jesus the whole world was jammed, pregnant, loaded, bulging with untapped, undiscovered, undetected POSSI-BILITIES! Jesus really believed in the supreme possibilities!

Man *can* be born again!

Character *can* be changed!

You *can* become a new person!

Life *can* be beautiful!

There *is* a solution to every problem!

There *is* a light behind every shadow!

Yes! Jesus had an unshakable faith in these ultimate possibilities:

God exists!

Life goes on beyond death!

Heaven is for real!

Jesus was prepared to prove it. By dying—and rising again!

"I'm a child of God!"

"I'm God's idea, and God only has good ideas!"

"I *want* to do it! I *can* do it! I *will* do it!"

"I'm going to take chances!"

A Matter of Trust

God gives his ideas to everyone. Yet some people close their ears to them, while others hear them but are afraid to act upon those ideas or to believe in them. Did you know that the difference between the super-success, the moderate-success, and the loser is not a matter of talent, training, or territory? It is a matter of trust.

Say "Yes!"

Never reject an idea because it's going to create problems or it's dangerous or risky.

Possibility thinking says, "Yes!" to an idea if it's going to help people who are in pain. It says "Yes!" to an idea if it holds the prospect of contributing to peace, prosperity, and pride in the human family.

When you say "Yes!" you will be living and trusting in God's promises. When you attempt the impossible you will discover that you will be filled with excitement! Enthusiasm! Energy! Youth! Happiness!

A Drive-In Church? Why Not!

It's been nearly twenty-five years since I buried Rosie Gray in a simple ceremony in a cemetery in the little town of El Toro, California.

I had started my church in that town in a drive-in theater, for want of a better place. And on the first Sunday a California rancher lifted his paralyzed wife into his car to take her to this new "drive-in" church. Then came the day when he telephoned me and asked me to call on his wife in their home.

I will never forget Warren Gray, her husband, meeting me outside his little ranch house and saying, "Reverend Schuller, before you meet my wife I must tell you something about her. You might think she does not have her senses, but her mind is perfect, absolutely perfect. She has had a stroke, and she cannot raise her head. She cannot close her eyes and she cannot move them; they simply stare ahead. Her head just stays on her chest. She cannot walk; she cannot talk. She can cry a little and grunt a little, but that is all."

I went into the house. She sat slumped in an old overstuffed chair, her head resting with her chin on her chest. Her eyes were open wide; they never blinked!

I knelt in front of her so my eyes could make contact with her, and I asked her, "Rosie, do you love Jesus?" A tear formed and rolled down her cheek.

"Rosie, do you want to be baptized?"

A couple more tears rolled down and she grunted, "Uh, uh, uh."

The following Sunday Warren parked their car in the front row of the drive-in. I attached a long drop cord to my microphone, walked over to her car, and, reaching through an open window, baptized her.

At that time our church was ready to move into a beautiful chapel that we had just built on two acres of land. What were we going to do now about Rosie Gray? The drive-in setting had been perfect for her needs.

The decision was made to have services at 9:30 in the new chapel. Then I would go back to the drive-in to preach to Rosie in her car. I would do that for her until she passed away. "That won't be long," we all thought. But she lived one year, two years, three years, four years, five years—she just would not die. Amazing!

Finally, God put into our minds His Dream for a most unusual church. Why not design a building where walls would open and people in their cars could join inside-the-church worshipers in prayer and praise?

So, we bought a larger piece of property and designed such a church. We had the groundbreaking ceremony on a Sunday. The local newspapers ran the story on Monday morning—the ground had been broken for what was called

the world's first walk-in, drive-in church. On that same afternoon I had a funeral...for Rosie Gray.

Today the Crystal Cathedral where my congregation meets has walls that open to drive-in worshipers. And I shall always know that our unique church would not be the way it is had it not been for Rosie Gray! She was a quiet, meek soul, but she had a big impact on the direction of my ministry.

It Began With a Kite String

"Let's build a bridge across Niagara," someone proposed nearly a century ago. Great idea, it would save miles and miles of travel and solve many problems. But how were they to begin? The canyon walls were too steep, and the rapids were too wild to get that first strand across from cliff to cliff. Then someone got a bright idea. They'd offer a ten-dollar prize to the kid who could fly a kite from one side to the other. That's how the first string got across. It was then connected to a slender cable. And the slender cable was connected to the strong cable that made the entire construction possible.

When the project was first announced, the critics laughed. When they heard that a "kite was going to solve the problem," the sophisticated engineers had a field day. Well, history had the last laugh. One young boy, Homan Walsh, flew the first string across the chasm with his kite in 1848. He succeeded, and the process worked just as it was envisioned. The boy collected his ten dollars; the great suspension bridge was started with a single string.

Do Something Beautiful for God

God's care will carry you
so you can
carry others!

Heaven is Right Now!

I am sure you have heard of Mother Teresa of Calcutta. She's been listed frequently in *Good Housekeeping* magazine's most-admired-women list. She is one of the most beautiful persons alive in the world today.

She has over ten thousand dying lepers in her colony. Her colonies have spread into twenty-eight cities, to Ceylon, to the Indian people who live in London, Rome, Venezuela, and Australia. She and all of those who are members of the Missionaries of Charity have taken the vow of total poverty. The only thing they may own is the cheapest cotton garment and a pair of sandals. Total surrender!

Malcolm Muggeridge, who interviewed Mother Teresa on the British Broadcasting Company and later visited her in Calcutta, said, "The thing I noticed about you and the hundreds of sisters who now form your team is that you all look so happy. Is it a put-on?" She said, "Oh no, not at all. Nothing makes you happier than when you really reach out in mercy to someone who is badly hurt."

Mother Teresa has written: "Joy. Joy is prayer. Joy is strength. Joy is love. God loves a cheerful giver. She gives most who gives joy. The best way to show my gratitude to God is to accept everything, even my problems, with joy. A

joyful heart is a normal result of a heart that is burning with love. Never let anything so fill you with sorrow as to make you forget for one moment the joy of Christ risen."

She goes on: "We all long for heaven, where God is. But we have it in our power to be in heaven with God right now, at this very moment. But to be at home with God now means loving the unlovely as He does, helping the helpless as He does, giving to those in need as He gives, serving the lonely as He serves, rescuing the perishing as He rescues. This is my Christ. This is the way I live."

God is so real. He will be real to you, too, if you take Christ into your heart. Adopt Mother Teresa's goal to "do something beautiful for God." Look around you now to help someone who is hurting. Do it for Christ's sake.

If you want a life-changing experience with God, a dynamic faith, here's how you can get it. Ask God to take your life, to heal the subconscious memories. Ask Jesus Christ to forgive you for your secret sins. Then ask Him to take your life and show you how you can be a part of something beautiful for God! For faith combined with good works makes God come alive within you.

Sow A Joyful Harvest

It is impossible to have thoughts of resentment and jealousy, anger and hate and ill-will—and be happy. You cannot sow these negative emotional seeds and expect to raise a harvest of smiles and laughter. Nobody can be happy and bitter at the same time. It is so incredibly simple. The secret to the prescription then is to care. Caring becomes carrying.

A Positive Chain

A dear friend of mine is Bill Dearden, chairman of the board of Hershey Foods Corporation. Bill was just a young boy back in the 1930s—an orphan. But he was fortunate to go to an orphan school started by Milton Hershey, the founder of the company.

Mr. Hershey had no children of his own, and he had a terrible time growing up himself. He only had a fourth-grade education. He failed three times in business ventures, but he had the courage to keep on trying. The fourth time he started in business—a caramel company—he was very successful.

He sold his caramel business for a million dollars and started the chocolate company. Knowing that his wife could never have any children, he decided to start an orphan school.

It was at this school that Bill Dearden received most of his education. He went on to work in the company and eventually became the chairman of the board. He tells me that Mr. Hershey set the company up so that 51% is owned by the school. So a lot of the money the company makes goes back into the school.

I asked Bill, "How did you make it from being a little orphan boy in the streets of Philadelphia to being the top corporate chief and chairman of the board of one of America's most respected corporations?"

He replied, "God has always had an important spot in my life. I believe that through His love and direction all things are

possible. I think He helped me along the way—guided me, and directed me—and I think He will do that for everyone if they are willing to believe in Him."

Mr. Hershey had a burning desire to do something good with his life. So did Bill Dearden. And so the positive chain of real righteousness goes on.

It's impossible to give anything away. Whatever you give away will always come back to you.

Love—An International Language

I met her during the six months my fourteen-year-old daughter was in the hospital recovering from the amputation of her leg after a terrible motorcycle accident. She was a refugee from Vietnam and did not speak English. She had the most menial job in the hospital—emptying the waste baskets. But each time she passed my daughter's bed, she'd stop and smile. Love radiated from her face, and that helped our feverish little girl. Love is the international language that builds self-esteem. No person is so ignorant, so uneducated, so lacking in talent or beauty that he or she is incapable of becoming a really love-sharing person.

The Prescription

The prescription for joyful living is very simple: If you want to be happy, treat people right. If you carry somebody else's burdens, in the process you'll discover the secret of happiness.

*Selfishness
turns life
into a burden.
Unselfishness
turns
burdens
into life!*

Turn Scars to Stars!

When God sees a
breach...
He builds a
bridge!

When He sees a
scar...
He creates a
star!

Forgiveness Heals

She is no longer with us—our dear Schug. Her name was Bernice Schug, but my children called her simply "Schug." Since both my wife's and my families lived in the Midwest, our children were unable to spend much time with their grandparents.

When we met Schug at church she was a widow. Her own grandchildren lived in northern California, so she was unable to see them as often as she liked. It was inevitable then that Schug would become our California grandmother. She lavished love and poppy-seed rolls on us and our children. She stayed over with the children when my wife had our last two children. She ate meals with us, she cared for our children, yet none of us knew how deep her hidden wound was.

One day Schug came to me and said, "Bob, I was reading in the church bulletin today that you are having a guest speaker next Sunday. I see you're having a Kamikaze pilot as your guest."

Oh! I remembered then that Schug's son had been killed in World War II by a Kamikaze pilot. "That's right, Schug. This particular pilot was trained as a Kamikaze and would have died as a Kamikaze had the war not ended when it did. But he has a tremendous story to tell of how he found Jesus."

"That may be. I don't think I will be in church that Sunday, though. I don't think I could handle it."

"I understand," I replied. "I don't think it will hurt if you miss one Sunday."

The next Sunday the Japanese pilot shared his story. His love and gratitude for Jesus shone from his eyes. You could feel the love and release he had found.

People were moved by his testimony. And when the service was over, my associate pastor walked with him back down the aisle to the rear of the church.

Suddenly as they approached the last pew, an older woman stepped out. She stood firmly in front of the Kamikaze pilot and blocked his exit. She looked at him squarely and said, "My son was killed in the war by a Kamikaze!"

It was Schug. We all held our breath as she continued, "God has forgiven you for your sins, and tonight He has forgiven me of mine."

She threw her arms around the Japanese pilot and hugged him and cried and cried as she released all the bitterness and anger that had been harbored for so many years.

Forgive a Kamikaze pilot, when a fellow pilot had killed a beloved son? Impossible! Yes, it is impossible for us, but not impossible for God!

"It's Not Fair!"

Here is an attitude that is a sure prescription for happiness. Learn to live by this refreshing, happy attitude: "It's not what happens to me that matters most; it's how I react to what happens to me."

Be sure of this: If you have the attitude that you should forever be spared from all pain, hurt, and grief, you can be positive that someday you will be jolted with a depressing disillusionment. Sorrow, rejection, bereavement hit all of us at some point in our lives. To expect that somehow we are privileged persons and should be immune from hurt and hardship is unrealistic.

Some even feel, "Because I am a Christian, I should experience no pain and suffering. Because I'm a God-fearing person and a good person, I should experience no rejection or ridicule." If this is our attitude, we will react to adversity with self-pity. "It's not fair!" will be our immediate negative reaction. But the quicker we learn that life is *not* always fair, the sooner we can achieve emotional maturity.

Father, we are so thankful to be together again for a time of fellowship.

We ask that this will be an enjoyable year of learning and sharing.

Thank you for our many blessings —

We ask these things in Jesus name — and we thank you Father — Amen

What is the cross?
It is a
minus

turned into a
plus!

Choose to be Happy—Anyway!

Do you feel persecuted? Then be of good cheer! You can choose to be happy—anyway. Yes! *You* can be happy, too, even if you are the innocent victim of authentic injustice, insult, injury, discrimination, or oppression.

How can you be happy when you are facing persecution? Is this really possible? Oh, yes. There are several people I know who have gone through tremendous suffering, and they have emerged from the fire not unscathed, but stronger.

These people who were able to be victorious because they:

1) *Remained POSITIVE!* They took a positive attitude—they chose to rejoice in spite of their circumstances.

2) *Were PREPARED!* They had equipped themselves with a spiritual and emotional support system that became an invisible shield.

3) *PERSEVERED in doing what is right.* They kept on keeping on, and would not let others get the better of them.

4) *PARDONED those who hurt them!* They forgave those who did the persecuting.

5) *PERSISTED in trusting God,* even when He seemed far away! They kept in mind that God is the ruler yet, that He will have the last word and it will be good.

6) *PRAYED for understanding and strength!* They accepted the help God offers to those that are suffering. They understood that they were not the only ones who had ever been persecuted, and so they resisted the temptation to fall victim to the persecution complex and martyr syndrome.

7) *PASSED triumphantly through the necessary PHASES* that we must all go through when we face tragedy!

A Salve for Hidden Wounds

Don't nurse the wound. Don't curse the wound. Don't keep rehearsing the wounding experience. What do you do with your hidden wounds? *Immerse them.* Drown them in a life of noble service.

I remember a time in the early years of my ministry when I had a real personal problem with someone. Sometimes it hurt me so badly I didn't know how to handle it. At these times my wife always had a solution. She'd say, "I think you ought to visit Marie; it was a year ago that her husband died."

So I would go out to the hospitals and I would go calling on people. I would immerse myself as a pastor in the hearts of people who were hurting. And in the process, my little hidden wound was just drowned to death. It up and died.

How do you handle your hidden wounds? Don't nurse them. Don't curse them. Don't rehearse them. Do immerse them. And finally, *reverse them*. Turn the negative into a positive. You do that when you allow your wound to turn you into a more sensitive, compassionate, considerate, thoughtful, merciful, gracious person.

If your wound is something that you can't share with others without criticizing somebody else or tearing him or her down, then you have to suffer in silence. If that's the case, then trust God. Let Him heal your hidden wounds.

Blessed are those whose dreams are shaped by their hopes... not by their hurts!

What happens
to
good people
when
bad things
happen
to them?

They become…
better
people!

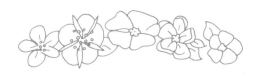

Make
Peace
on
Earth

*"God Loves You
And So Do I"*

*...a prescription
for peacemaking*

God's Call

On the morning of my ordination as a minister, I opened my Bible for my devotions. It fell open to this passage: "You shall be called the repairer of the breach, the restorer of paths to dwell in" (Isa. 58:12). And I adopted this Bible verse as a direction from my Lord to try to promote a peaceful resolution to any conflict I see. Peacemaking has been one of the important goals of my ministry.

I believe that all of us are called to try to be peacemakers. And being a peacemaker can be extremely rewarding. Helping bring peace where there is tension and conflict and strife brings about a healthy sense of satisfaction, self-esteem, self-worth.

"I am The Vine"

God chooses us to serve His purpose. "You did not choose me, but I chose you." Our self-esteem is rooted in our divine call. God's dream for our life and work gives purpose and pride to our life. Our role is clear; we are to be the branches of Christ's love in the world, "I am the vine, you are the branches."

Clean Up!

If there is a negative emotion within you that is blocking you in your relationship with God, *clean up!* Here are some exercises to help you:

1) Think of some hidden hurt in your past and pray a forgiving prayer for the person who was the cause of your hurt. C. S. Lewis said it: "We all agree that forgiveness is a beautiful idea until we have to practice it!"

2) Think of someone of whom you are jealous, and pray for that person's continued prosperity.

3) Think of someone you've hurt, cheated, insulted, slighted, snubbed, or criticized. Call him or her. Invite this person to have dinner or lunch with you. Confess to him or her your un-Christian attitude, and ask for forgiveness.

4) Think of some neglected cause, project, or person. Surprise yourself with a streak of generosity! Really give a lot—of yourself and of your substance.

5) Pray a totally honest prayer to Christ. You doubt God? Tell Him so. He'll still love you, even if you don't believe in Him! (God specialized in loving sinners!)

Meet the "Prince of Peace"

Do you want peace in your family? Do you want peace in your community? Do you want peace with other races and other cultures? There will not be peace anywhere as long as there is a war going on in your heart and in your soul.

So how do you make peace with yourself? You make peace with yourself by meeting the greatest peacemaker of all time, Jesus Christ. He was called "the Prince of Peace." He lived, He died on a Friday we call Good Friday, and He rose again on Easter. He's alive today. He is your closest personal friend.

Those Two Little Words

Oh, the power of those restorative words, "I'm sorry!" They heal relationships—between ourselves and our friends and loved ones, and between ourselves and our Lord.

The psalmist wrote, "A broken and contrite heart, O God, thou wilt not despise" (Ps. 51:17).

He wrote for many. Throughout the Scriptures we see them—the broken and contrite:

The penitent thief

The prodigal son

David, the adulterer

Saul of Tarsus, a murderer of Christians

Mary Magdalene, the prostitute

These scalawags—what do they all have in common? They all belong to God's Hall of Fame. In the corridors of heaven they all have positions of honor.

How did they acquire such noble recognition? All of them reached a point in their personal shortcomings, sin, and shame when they cried out, "O God, be merciful to me, a sinner!"

We Are One Family

Why should we make every effort to be as successful as we can? Why should we strive to achieve the most that we can? Why should we sacrifice to be all that we can be? Why must we build bridges? Why must we be peacemakers? Why must we compromise, again and again, in order to try to understand those who are our antagonists? The answer is simple. We must do these things so as not to stain or soil the good name of our heavenly Father whose family name we claim by his grace.

Why must we spend all of our efforts to tell the whole world about Jesus Christ? Why must we spare nothing to share the good news of each person's worth? Again, we must, because we want the entire human family to become a brotherhood and so live that we are proud of ourselves. Then, and only then, will the Father be glorified.

Positive Humility

Humility doesn't mean to put yourself down, to say, "I'm no-body. I can't do it." That's not humility. It may be the projection of an inferiority complex. But real humility is not self-denigration. Real humility is the awareness that there are others who can help you. Real humility is also the capacity to say, "I was wrong; you were right."

Bring Out the Best

Service is its own reward. A prescription for joyful living is: "Be good, be kind, be unselfish. Do unto others as you would have them do unto you."

If you want positive things to happen, you must be positive. If you want to be friendly with people and if you want people to be friendly toward you, be friendly to them. If you are surrounded by undesirable people, change them into good people.

How do you change them into good people? Bring the best out of them! How do you bring the best out of them? Call attention to the best that is within them! Until they begin to believe they are beautiful people, they will not treat you beautifully.

Help
Inner
Happiness
Happen!

If we hunger and thirst after positive attitudes, hard work, knowledge, and excellence, the odds of our winning rise astronomically.

Who's Perfect?

A perfect farm, a profitable farm, a righteous farm is not a farm where there are no weeds growing. Rather, it is the farm that's planted with crops such as corn or pineapple and is bearing fruit.

A perfect sheet of paper isn't a sheet of paper that has no mark on it, without scratch or flaw. No. The perfect paper is one that is filled with notes, thoughts, concepts, and ideas—a poem, an outline, or numbers that put together some creative possibility.

A perfect communication between two people isn't the type of relationship in which there are no fights, no arguments, no cross words. Perfect communication is when both persons are able to open up and actually tell each other how they feel, with respect and mutual esteem. Not silence, but

creative, constructive, respectful conversation is righteousness in communication.

I would advise parents not to be afraid to be transparent with their children. Show them your weaknesses. Don't give them the impression you're perfect. Don't create shoes so large that your child will never be able to fill them. Be open, too. Share with them the predicament you find yourself in as a parent. Ask your teenager, "How would you handle this problem if you were the father or the mother?"

Be open. Be humble. Correctable. Educable. Then you will hear God's voice. You will see God's plan. Grab onto it, give it all you've got, and you will inherit the earth!

Want to be Popular?

What is the essence of self-esteem? It's knowing that I have done my best and I am recognized and honored as a child of God!

What do people think of me? How we handle this human question is extremely important. So many of us think of it in terms of being "popular."

But I am not really thinking about popularity here—or at least, not *that* kind of popularity. Unless you can maintain an honorable reputation you will not have the kind of popularity that will leave you with a wholesome and healthy sense of self-esteem! The young person who resists the temptation

to do drugs feels victorious. He has been a winner! He has been the strongest! He feels good about himself. And such a person will eventually build a positive reputation.

The goal is not just to be popular—but to be popularly recognized as a beautiful human being—a child of God!

Our attitude shouldn't be: "I don't care what people say."

Our attitude shouldn't be: "I want to be popular at any price."

Our attitude should be: "I will strive so to live that I shall build a reputation as a beautiful child of God!"

We Always Have A Choice

Dr. Viktor Frankl, an eminent psychiatrist and author of the famous book, *Man's Search for Meaning,* is a living example of our freedom of choice.

Dr. Frankl, who is a Jew, was imprisoned by the Nazis in the Second World War. His wife, his children, and his parents were all killed in the holocaust.

The Gestapo took Viktor and made him strip. He stood there totally naked. But they noticed that he still had on his wedding band. As they removed even that from him, he said to himself, "You can take away my wife, you can take away my children, you can strip me of my clothes and my freedom, but there is one thing no person can ever take away from me— and that is my freedom to choose how I will react to what happens to me!"

We are free to choose our attitude in any given situation—to maintain a positive attitude no matter how negative the situation. What a life-changing idea!

Let Your Joy Flow!

There was a time when my children were little that I was going through some torturing times with the development of my church. I had colossal burdens and pressures. And although I was going through the motions of being a pastor, a husband, and a father, my heart was not really in any of these. It was blocked by despair, depression, and fear.

One day my wife and I were walking through the garden. I remarked, "Honey, the roses are blooming." To my surprise, she replied, "They've been blooming for three months."

It was not until I cried out to God and asked Him to release me from my anxieties and worries that I was able once more to feel His presence. Like a finger pressing into my brain, He touched me, and I felt the fear and the despair drain out of me. In its place flowed peace, joy, and hope, despite the obstacles that still lay ahead.

When God touched me, my ears were opened. I could once again hear what my family was saying to me. My eyes were opened. I could once again see the beauty that God had created. I could even see possible solutions for the overwhelming problems I was facing.

Happiness Is...

Happiness—that deep inner strength that is made up of courage, faith, hope, and peace. Mix them together, and you have happiness!

Happiness—the courage to hang on in the face of severe adversity!

Happiness—the faith that God will have the last word, and it will be good!

Happiness—the hope that, even though you can only see the shadow, someday the clouds will clear away and the sun will shine again!

Happiness—the quiet sense of self-esteem that comes when you know you have done your best.

Happiness—the assurance that you have been merciful and kind to enemy and friend alike.

Happiness—the quiet assurance that God will be merciful and kind to you, too.

Happiness—the beautiful belief that this life, no matter how difficult it may be, is not your final destination.

*God will have
the last word*

*and it will be
…Good!*

Edited by Stephanie C. Oda
Book Design by Holly Johnson
Typeset in Zapf Chancery Medium Italic and Aldus
Cover design by Robert Pantelone
Cover photograph by Ed Cooper